SOLAR SYSTEM MISSION

Francis Spencer

A Crabtree Seedlings Book

Table of Contents

A Home in the Milky Way Galaxy 4
The Sun 9
Eight Planets 12
Dwarf Planets 20
Beyond Neptune 22
Glossary 23
Index 23

A Home in the Milky Way Galaxy

The Milky Way **Galaxy** is made up of gas, dust, and billions of stars and solar systems.

The Milky Way is just one of billions of galaxies in the universe.

A force called gravity holds the Milky Way together.

Our **solar system** is in the Milky Way Galaxy. In the center of our solar system is a star we call the Sun.

The Sun

The Sun is made up of burning gases.

We need the Sun for heat and light.

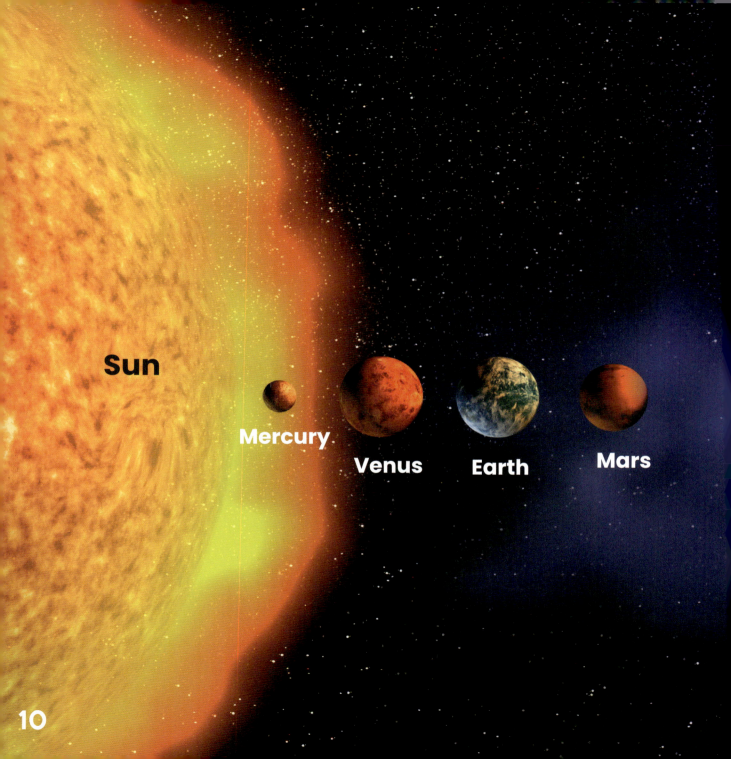

The Sun's gravity keeps the planets in our solar system in their **orbits**.

There are eight planets in our solar system.

Eight Planets

The four planets closest to the Sun are rocky planets. Their solid, rocky surfaces can take the Sun's heat.

Like all the rocky planets, Mercury has a rocky outer layer and a metal **core**.

Mercury is the smallest planet in our solar system.

Venus is about the same size as Earth. Like Mercury, Venus does not have a moon.

Venus is the hottest planet in our solar system.

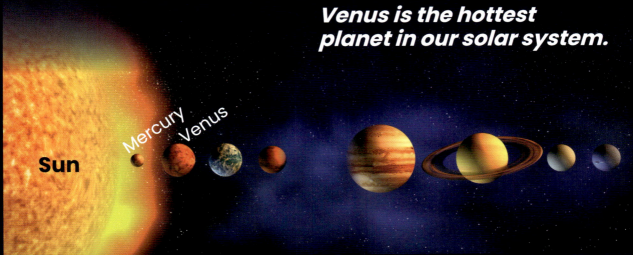

Sun · Mercury · Venus

13

Earth is the third planet from the Sun. Almost three quarters of Earth is covered in water.

Earth has one moon.

It takes Earth 365 days, or one year, to travel once around the Sun.

14

Mars is the fourth rocky planet. It looks red because it is covered in a rusted iron dust. Mars has two moons.

NASA sends robotic vehicles to Mars to take photos and gather information.

Sun Earth Mars

The next two planets, Jupiter and Saturn, are made mostly of gases. We call these two planets gas giants.

Jupiter is the largest planet in our solar system. Jupiter has 79 known moons.

Jupiter's Great Red Spot is a giant storm twice the size of Earth!

It is easy to remember Saturn because of its rings. Saturn has 53 moons. It may have 29 more, which scientists are still learning about.

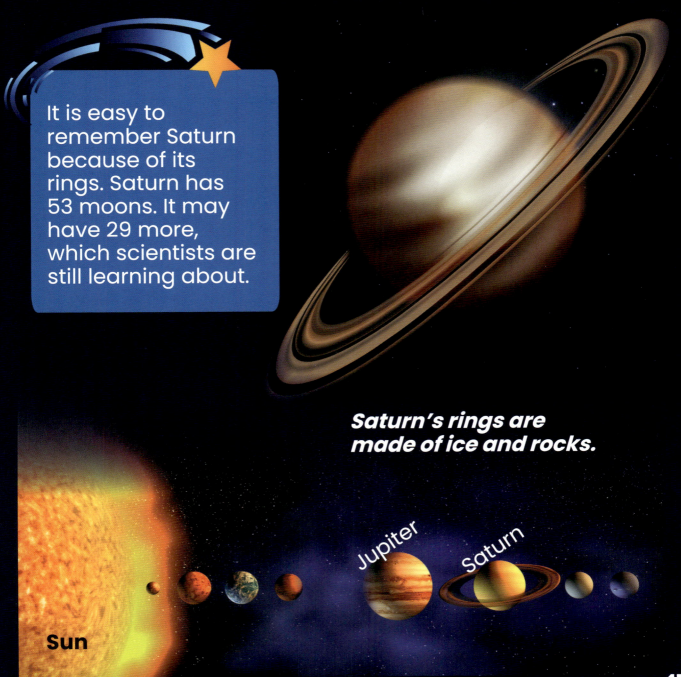

Saturn's rings are made of ice and rocks.

Sun
Jupiter
Saturn

Uranus and Neptune are also made mostly of gases. Because most of their gases are frozen, we call these two planets ice giants.

Uranus also has rings, but they are harder to see than Saturn's rings. Uranus has 27 known moons.

Uranus spins on its side.

Neptune is the windiest planet in our solar system. It has 14 known moons.

It takes Neptune about 165 Earth years to travel once around the Sun!

Dwarf Planets

Dwarf planets are too small to be true planets. They also share their orbits with other space objects. True planets do not share their orbits.

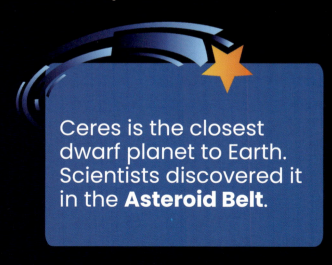

Ceres is the closest dwarf planet to Earth. Scientists discovered it in the **Asteroid Belt**.

These are the five named dwarf planets. Scientists think we will find many more.

Beyond Neptune

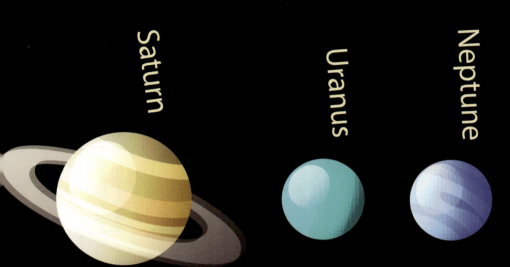

Just beyond Neptune is the **Kuiper Belt**—a ring of icy rocks, comets, and other space objects.

Beyond the Kuiper Belt, scientists believe there is a giant cloud of icy objects.

Glossary

Asteroid Belt (ASS-tuh-royd BELT): A ring of millions of rocks between the orbits of Mars and Jupiter.

core (KOR): The center or innermost layer.

galaxy (GAL-uhk-see): Gas, dust, and billions of stars and their solar systems held together by gravity.

Kuiper Belt (KYE-per BELT): A ring of icy rocks and space objects outside of Neptune's orbit.

orbits (OR-bits): Invisible paths that planets travel.

solar system (SOH-lur SISS-tuhm): A star and all the planets and space objects that orbit it.

Index

asteroid(s) 20
gas(es) 4, 9, 16, 18
Earth 8, 10, 13-16, 19, 20

Milky Way (Galaxy) 4, 5, 7
rocky 12, 15
solar system(s) 4, 7, 11, 12, 13, 16, 19

star(s) 4, 7
Sun 6-15, 17, 19

School-to-Home Support for Caregivers and Teachers

This book helps children grow by letting them practice reading. Here are a few guiding questions to help the reader build his or her comprehension skills. Possible answers appear here in red.

Before Reading

- **What do I think this book is about?** I think this book is about the solar system that includes Earth. I think this book is about all the planets that are in our solar system.

- **What do I want to learn about this topic?** I want to learn about the Milky Way Galaxy and where it got its name. I want to learn which planet is closest to the Sun and which is the farthest away.

During Reading

- **I wonder why…** I wonder why the four planets closest to the Sun are called rocky planets. I wonder why Earth is covered with so much water.

- **What have I learned so far?** I have learned that Mars is the fourth planet from the Sun. I have learned that Mars has two moons.

After Reading

- **What details did I learn about this topic?** I have learned that Jupiter and Saturn are the two planets that are made mostly of gases. I have learned that Jupiter is the largest planet in our solar system.

- **Read the book again and look for the glossary words.** I see the word *galaxy* on page 4, and the words *solar system* on page 7. The other glossary words are found on page 23.

Library and Archives Canada Cataloguing in Publication

CIP available at Library and Archives Canada

Library of Congress Cataloging-in-Publication Data

CIP available at Library of Congress

Crabtree Publishing Company
www.crabtreebooks.com   1-800-387-7650

Print book version produced jointly with Blue Door Education in 2022

Content produced and published by Blue Door Education, Melbourne Beach FL USA. This title Copyright Blue Door Education. All rights reserved. No part of this book may be reproduced or utilized in any form or by any means, electronic or mechanical including photocopying, recording, or by any information storage and retrieval system without permission in writing from the publisher.

PHOTO CREDITS:
Cover ©bobboz, star graphic on most pages ©Gleb Guralnyk; page 2-3 © Vadim Sadovski; page 5 ©Chanwit Ohm, page 6 © Christos Georghiou, pages 8-9 © bobboz, pages 10-11 and as an inset on pages 13, 15, 17, 19 ©Orla, page 12 ©otted Yeti, page 14 (Earth) ©Koyso Studio, (moon) ©Aphelleon, page 15 (Mars) ©Nerthuz, (Rover) ©Triff, page 16 © Dotted Yeti, page 17 © JuliRose, page 18 ©Vadim Sadovski, page 22 ©shooarts All images from Shutterstock.com except: page 13 (Venus), 19 and 21 courtesy of NASA.

Written by: Francis Spencer
Production coordinator and Prepress technician: Tammy McGarr
Print coordinator: Katherine Berti

Printed in the U.S.A./CG20210915/012022

Published in the United States
Crabtree Publishing
347 Fifth Ave.
Suite 1402-145
New York, NY 10016

Published in Canada
Crabtree Publishing
616 Welland Ave.
St. Catharines, Ontario
L2M 5V6